# THE UNDONE HEART

The Aim of work is more than the exchange of goods and services. It is the outer expression of an inner life.

You are the 'soul' agent qualified for This transaction.

Ty

# THE UNDONE HEART

## TYRONE HOLMES

ISBN: 0692786864
ISBN 13: 9780692786864

# TABLE OF CONTENTS

# ACKNOWLEDGMENTS

Thank you to every single person who has taken the time to teach me something about love. While you are all very precious to me, there are far too many of you to list here. So forgive me for singling out a select few.

Mom and Dad, my childhood was pure magic. I am so grateful for the way you loved my sister and I but I am even more grateful for the way you loved each other. I often feel that it will take several lifetimes to master the loving wisdom that filled my childhood home.

Tanya, my sweet sister, thank you for your relentless kindness. I am proud to be your brother. I adore and admire you.

Rudrani Farbman Brown, my dear teacher, you changed my life. Thank you for introducing me to the path of yoga. My heart, my mind and my life are still being transformed in immeasurable ways by the teachings, the time and the wisdom you have shared.

Ella and Maya my beautiful girls, I love you. I could not ask for two more amazing daughters. Thank you for persistently introducing me to the unmapped regions of my own heart. You are my greatest teachers and I am humbled, honored and grateful to be your father. There is an abundance of peace, love, joy, courage, humor, intelligence, kindness and warmth within you both. It is my highest hope that your lives be both an exploration and an offering of these innate treasures. I love you with all my heart.

My beloved wife Jodi, I adore you. The moment we met, you set my soul on fire and changed the trajectory of my life. Our love has so completely consumed me that I scarcely remember who I was before we met. I cherish you more than I can say. Thank you for being my constant ally and my muse.

Warning: the following material contains poetry that will grip your busy mind by the reins and surrender it to your joy-filled heart.

These words, like honeybees, provide a stinging defense against mental misery and will pollinate your life with beauty.

Side effects include a deepening sense of connection, peace, and nourishment on a soul-u-lar level.

It would seem that
once again
love
has had its way with me
and left behind this verse

In honor of our night together...

# FELLOW
# DETECTIVES

I'm an atheist when my eyes open,
a believer when they close.
I blink all the time.

Poetry draws me inward
and decodes the beauty outside.

But the great mystery still eludes
me.

I claim no sovereignty over the truth;
it's all beyond the powers of my mind.

I just look for clues.
Love is my favorite.

When I find it, I shout
so my fellow detectives can hear.

And I hope you'll do the same for me.

# THE GREAT REVEAL

This is not a book.
It is a map
of the valley
of the Secret One.

These are not poems.
They are medicine
for the only human ailment.

Life has ached so tenderly
since the night
of the
great reveal,

Since the invitation
was issued
to let go of
want.

In the valley
of the Secret One

A circle of
Presence

provides protection
from the torment
of thought.

A ring of fire
burns pain

While eagle talons
clutching
bags of smoke
carry it away.

Trees stand counsel,
whispering wisdom
among the leaves.

Like a hungry lover,
silence invades every
pore.

Sweet messages pour forth
in the moonlight,
saying,
"Rest, love.
Put down the compass."

These are not words;
they are bread crumbs

Left
for those
selfless enough to follow
the path of
cosmic joy,

Left for those
brave enough
to call this valley,

To call this space
that irradiates
and utterly eviscerates fear,

Home.

# MYSTIC HEART

Mystic heart,
try to understand
why
they turn red
and look away
in
your presence,

For you have fallen too in love
with heaven
to choose an angel,
when your Beloved lives
as every form.

That kind of naked longing,
that kind of adultery,
makes the monogamous
blush.

# ANGELS CRY

I cannot explain
what
this is doing to my heart,

The full depths of which
are beyond understanding

But fill me with an
ecstatic joy
that has brought me to the precipice
of madness.

And from the chasm
I hear a chorus of angels cry,
"Jump, dear boy,
jump."

# APPROACH THE BENCH

If your mind makes you sick
with its wicked
counsel,

If his ill-crafted advice
increases your
despair,

If his defense costs you dearly
and his closing arguments
never cease,

Do not cast off your gifts in
an attempt to flee Her Majesty's
court.

Instead,
dear one,
change
lawyers.

# UNCONQUERABLE GRATITUDE

The Divine is hard to find
in this world,
with Her damn
omnipresence.
Everywhere is, after all,
the best hiding place.
But I have a secret,

A way to recognize Her
amid Her many forms.

You see,
royalty always wears a crown
so that Her wild lovers won't
mistake Her for a commoner.

A crown of
unconquerable gratitude
will adorn
the gaze of all those
whose hearts are inhabited
by the Beloved.

When you see these
humbling lights,

Brace yourself,

For you are standing
on the front porch
of Jah.

# SAFE PASSAGE

Actions
born of ignorance
are like stones
resting
in the dark recesses
of our soul's past.

It hurts
to see them
under the blazing
light of spiritual wisdom.

But in time
we see that they
create a safe passage,

For they are coverings that
keep us from
falling again
in the same holes.

So, as you travel
by them,
instead of seeing
imperfections,
mistakes,
and diminished nobility,

Instead of being
absorbed in the
intense gravitational pull
of regret,

Understand them
as disciplined
guideposts

Paid for with the
currency
of life experience,

Pointing you in
the direction
of freedom.

# THE CLEARING SPACE

Sometimes, the Beloved becomes
a book we read,
a course we take,
a practice we keep.

Erroneously, we think nothing of it,
for our eyes are blind to
the movement of air.

But the heart senses
the Presence
clearing space,
gently blowing away
the accumulated dust,
one bunny at a time.

We want faster change,
but few lovers can bear
a tornado.

# EVERY SAINT

Every saint carries
a two-sided coin in
his or her heart.

Heads:
there is no man-made
boundary in existence
that can withstand
the omnipresent flow of love.

Tails:
every boundary to love
in existence
is man-made.

And they walk the earth
tirelessly,
flipping their coins and
sharing the wealth.

# SANCTUARY

The heart is sanctuary,

A place of rest from the torments
of the mind.

The wise
don't just vacation there,

They take up permanent
residence.

# FEARLESSLY FORGIVING

Somedays, we're madmen who grab
joy by the throat and bury her,
battered alive.

Somedays, we're archaeologists
excavating light from the ruins of our
shattered lives.

I don't need a calendar for the days
of the week. I know by the look in your
eyes.

No need to speak.
Love is
fearlessly forgiving
and ready
for any
surprise.

# DIVINE WILL

From the lips of the lazy,
the phrase
"It is all Divine Will"
can be a religious cop-out,
meaningless and trivial,
revealing nothing.

But
in the heart of the wise

It is a war cry
chanted silently,

Silently,

By soldiers who have been
wounded by love and
had the courage
to stand their ground
and return
fire.

# ONE

There is only one
Wisdom Tradition,

And love is her teacher,
the universe is her classroom,
and existence is her star
pupil.

# THE TIRE MARK

The master was world renowned and highly sought after.
The pupil asked, "Can you explain your apparent effect on people?"
To which the master replied,

"I was run over by God.
And since I was shirtless
at the time,
the tire mark is on my
skin for all to see.

"Since then,
everyone who sees me
strips naked
and
lies down in the street."

# JOINS IN

Children on fire with
the fuel of life

Run inside the house.
They scream,
they dance,
they shout,
they stomp.

The practical parent yells,
"Stop!
Be silent,
be still,"

while the Beloved secretly
joins in.

# THE DIFFERENCE

We are cups
made of water
born in an ocean,
you and I.

But for some
perplexing reason,
you are afraid
to spill.

# THE YOU WHO SEES

Students were gathered around the teacher.
One student said,
"I dreamed of peace. I was moving
or maybe the world was moving around me.
But wherever I looked,
there was peace.
Peace on the streets,
peace in the buildings, peace in trees, peace in the fields.
I was surrounded by it."

The teacher replied,
"And where were you in this dream?"

The student said,
"Well, I
was there.
In the center of it all."

The teacher asked,
"Could you see yourself?"

Student:
"Yes."

Teacher:
"Could you see your back and your face?"

Student:
"*Seeing* is not the right word.
It's more like I was aware of myself.
But yes, I could see my whole body."

Teacher:
"If you can see yourself in a dream,
then where is the you
who sees?"

The student considered this for a minute and answered.
"Everywhere."

Teacher:
"What...what is
this you, you speak of?
This you
who is everywhere?

"Furthermore,
which is more real?
The you who sees
yourself seeing the world,
or the you
being seen?"

Pondering this,
the student went away for forty years.

When he returned, his teacher asked,
"So, which you is the real you?"

The student replied,
"If you create two when there is one,
you create boundaries when there are none."

The teacher nodded.

Just then, some old classmates wandered by. One said,
"I can't believe it's been forty years since we have seen you!"

To which the teacher said,
"A woman carries a baby for nine months.

"There is no set gestation period
for birthing the
Buddha."

# ZOMBIE CONTAGION

There is a zombie contagion that eats the areas of the brain responsible for compassion and higher wisdom.
No one is immune.
*No one.*

It's hard to know who is infected because the symptoms manifest in ways suitable to the unique disposition of the host.
Most zombies don't know what's happening to them.
Many of the infected are unaware.

Unlike most zombie infections,
this one—*prejudice*—
is not spread by blood
or other bodily fluids.
It's much worse than that.
It's spread by thoughts.
Someone, somewhere, in our shared history was infected by a really dangerous idea: our physical and cultural differences were enough to split one human race into several.
This idea has been manipulated time and time again for the gain of a select few.

It's strengthened by fear, ignorance, and hatred.
It is cured only by love.

Some say that we are all unknowingly infected with one strain or another, making humanity hopelessly incurable.
But I disagree.

I have heard tales.
I have heard tales of people remembering their shared humanity, risking their lives for groups they didn't physically belong to. The infected cannot do that!

I have heard tales of infected grandparents expressing
that confused look of disbelief at the joy inspired by their multiracial grandchild.

I have heard stories of soldiers who've exhibited symptoms for years, finding brotherhood overseas with men they were taught to fear at home.

I have seen children
in diverse neighborhoods
raised together
relatively
contagion free.
I have even seen the infected repent and become healthy again.

While aggression is an understandable response to a
zombie outbreak,
we must be vigilant.
Studies show that any attempt to physically, intellectually, or emotionally harm the infected only spreads the sickness.

And just to be clear, today, right here at home, we are in the midst
of another outbreak.
Hate spreads it.
Love cures it.

Throughout time, there have been many outbreaks. Truthfully, our
nation was infected from the beginning.
But with each outbreak came a brave, strong, loving resistance intent on healing the planet of this plague. Unfortunately, this infection is tricky.
It adapts very well. When beaten back, it goes into hiding, mutates,
and emerges again stronger than before, manifesting itself through
new names, new faces, new policies, and new laws.

Each new outbreak is a call to action,
a reminder to finish the work of the former generation. We must
have faith that love will defeat this most recent outbreak. The publicity and attention it is receiving will subside. But we've learned
that nothing short of a complete global inoculation will do. If even
one zombie is left unhealed, the infection will repopulate the planet with frightening speed.

To those willing to continue this good work, humanity is depending on you. Your task is to blanket the planet with love, to commit to a daily and persistent practice of love work, and to cure every system known to man—school, political, religious, corporate, nervous, and circulatory.

Segregation is an incubator for infection. So, we need love workers in every suburb, farm, city, street corner, and gated community! *Never ever stop.*
This will be tiring. This will be downright exhausting. But it is completely necessary. And if you feel hostility growing within, if you start to feel dazed and confused, if you find yourself holding beliefs about one group or another, if you feel yourself looking at your fellow humans with disdain,
seek shelter and call for qualified help.
You yourself may be infected. Whatever you do, don't lash out. Instead, reach inward
for the cure.

# DIRECT ROUTE

Come,
stand against each other until
you are smooth.

Give each rough edge a sandpaper caress.
Let every odd protuberance be
filed down

So that the illusion of separation
slides off.

Leave ignorance nothing to cling to.

Come,
let transparency emerge
from your very skin
so that the Great Tenderness
can be viewed without obstruction.

Brothers and sisters, it does seem
safer to walk alone,
but please
do not be troubled.

Friction is simply
love's chauffeur,
chosen so that the
passenger is protected from
all who place the word
*me*
over
*we*.

And love—
she knows where she's going.

Love is alive in us and in the spaces between us.
And it is because of love's power
that we are
forever bound to one another,
forever held in gravity's embrace.

Love is a living bond
so powerful
that she obliterates all paths
that dare lead away from her.

Love cannot be divided, reduced, or contained.
Thought itself is but a simple servant,
trying desperately to appease
the majestic ruler of the heart.

So, slip on your shoes
and hop in.

Your destination?
The corner of Bliss
and U Street.

Buckle up. There are
no rest stops,
and never mind the tolls.

Sure, there may be traffic
from time to time.

But how else
should two travel
to become one

When marriage is such a perfectly
direct route?

# EXPERIENCE

There is a place,
a small peninsula
where the
seeds of interpretation
cannot flourish,

A realm where
judgement and distance,
the parents of opinion,
never met.

Maybe it's the altitude,
too much exposure
to the blazing light of
awareness.

There is no one map
to this place
because its location
is unique to every explorer.

A guide can point
the way,

But you must
go it alone.

The name of
this strange land…

The wise call it
Direct Experience.

# SILENCE AND SALT

Unearthed hypocrisy
is salt
poured on an
unknown wound

And then thinking,
"How long has this
been here?"

First the wound,
then the salt,
then the wondering.

The salt was a gift.
It shed light on the wound.

There was an ideal
you failed to master.

Ego-burning friction
often presents itself
as frustration.

We are all in need
of a good smoldering
sometimes.
The smoke sends a message
beyond.

We can't know what
the Friend hears.

Perhaps burning the
dross away allows
the Friend to hear
Herself.

But most wish the friction away,
unable to bear the burning.

At your command,
frustration flows
outward into the garden,
looking for delicate leaves to scorch.

The heat of your attention,
magnetically drawn
to the actions
of others.

Those leaves contain
aloe,
but they can't share it
now.

No, no.
This is not
the way.

For the humble,
there is only
salt,
silence and salt,
and then

Realization.

# USELESS

I can't force a
poem.

Whenever I try,
I realize
that the mind
is nothing more than
a microphone
for the heart,

Brilliant technology
but useless
without
the
voice.

# GRIP ON REALITY

When every being
becomes literate in the
language of the soul
and realizes that the whole
of existence is
nothing more than love,

Time
may
quite possibly develop
an inferiority complex
and an identity crisis
and, if we are lucky,
eventually
lose its grip
on reality.

# COMMENCEMENT CEREMONY

Goals,
schedules,
achievement.

Your mind,
like a polite student,
approaches these
with shirt properly tucked
and shoes polished,
hoping to receive an A
on life's report card.

Fool!

Your birth was
the final exam.

Your first breath was
the commencement ceremony.

And you toil daily,
waiting for your worth to be graded?

Go.
You're wasting time.

Life is a prom.

Don't keep
your heart—
that sweet, tender,
love-drunk beauty—
waiting
one second longer

For a dance with you.

# TREASURE MAP

You think me insane,
but
we are both pirates,
you and I.
Treasure maps in hand.
Mine was made by a Perfect One;
yours, a rich man.

This is why you built the finest ship
and search the whole world,

And I sit,
eyes closed,
alone
in darkness.

# BEWARE

Beware of that kind of love;
exhaustion quivers and runs
from it,
fear evaporates,
anger becomes a sobbing child,
and stress loses bodily control.

Beware of that kind of
love
that will destroy all that
you think you are,
leave you with nothing,
and
give you everything.

# PUT IT DOWN

Are you still holding a grudge
against those who have blown the lid
off your self-delusion?

Against those who have taken your
image and carelessly smashed it to
pieces?

Are you still demonizing those
who have uncovered your anger, greed,
and petty desires
and put them on display in the town square?

The blind often find the first taste of light painful and disorienting,
but no one upon finding this condition
reversed ever harbored anger toward the doctor
or foolishly asked to be put back
in the dark.

# ANY GOOD ATTORNEY

So, the facts of the case are these.
You don't control
space or time,

And yet all these wondrous
things get done.

Entire worlds are created,
galaxies spin at just
the right speed,
and somehow
it all works
in your favor.

Any good attorney would ask
the plaintiff,
"So,
how long have you and
eternity been lovers?"

# NOVEL SIZED

Poets are literary
magicians,

For they can pack
novel-sized truths
into a mere sentence.

# THE SANITARIUM

After being given
breath,
a heartbeat,
a body,
a mind,
and an entire world,

The patient continues
to demand credit
for everything.

The healers chant
one mantra
in the sanitarium:

"Nothing
is ever
done
alone."

# CHASTITY

Poverty is man-made.

Unlike bacteria,
which proliferates
on its own,

Poverty must be sustained
by man.

These thoughts
lift the mirror
that shame shoves
under the bed.

Abundance is
life's unique signature
on the world
that our blind denial
renders a forgery.

The mirror lights the way;
it clarifies the space
between each eyebrow,

The space
between want and need,
between fear and trust.

When the object of desire
becomes less interesting
than the source,

That small one within us
who lusts for individual wealth
will be humbled
into a state
of endless
chastity.

# BLOODLINE

Yesterday,
awareness so loved itself
that it burst in sound.

Sound vibrated so fast that
it exploded into light.

Light so loved its essence that
it crystalized into matter.

Matter, mad with desire, smashed
into itself and grew, then
reached across the heavens
to caress itself in form.

What started as flirtation
grew into full-blown ecstasy.

Unable to keep this
transgression quiet,
a litter of cells popped up
everywhere.

Yearning caused them to cluster tighter
and tighter together.

Today,
your brain, through awareness,
sends signals in the form of light impulses,
which contract or relax the heart,
whose beats pump
tightly clustered blood cells
around the body.

Dear ones,
how is it that
you still fail to
recognize
your parents

When you look so much alike?

# MEDITATION

Meditation—
The whole practice
can be summed up this way.

Be quiet.
I can't hear
the Beloved
with all
this
chatter.

Be still.
I can't see
the Friend
when you
flail around
so.

Be...

Be.

# TEENAGE LOVE

Service
is what happens
when you see
your
Beloved
everywhere
and
you just can't
keep your hands
to yourself.

# WHAT COMMIT MEANS

We stand on feet
that we did not build.

We walk on legs that
we do not own.

To commit
requires
first
to admit

That we are in the flow
of the great wave

And
second
to simply swim
without resistance
in
its direction.

# SO MUCH MORE

It is so much more
than this.

It is so much more than the
curve of your body that I am after,
much more than the exchange
of breath.

Heaven left a song inside you
that I am desperate to
find.

And when I hear it,
once and for all,
I will understand
love.

# BEDTIME ROUTINE

Should I behave like this?
Like a child demanding one more treat,
promising to be your best friend?

Should I behave like this?
Like a little one demanding one more
story before bed?

We all behave like this
until we hear Her
whisper that She will never ever leave.

Then, we explode in a raucous, whirling dance
that threatens to birth
another galaxy.

Only then can we rest,
stretch, yawn,
sleep, live…in peace.

# CHOSEN
# LANGUAGE

God is humble.

Imagine for a moment that you
were all powerful, omnipotent, and omnipresent.

Imagine that you were the creator of life, of all things, of all the
worlds.

God does all this
and permits us
to forget Him

So that we might experience
the vast richness of life

And even
if only for a moment
have the joy of remembrance.

There is no greater humility.
There is no love like that in all the worlds.

So, we are encouraged to be humble
before God,

Not for fear of punishment

But because humility is the
chosen language
spoken by the
Beloved Herself.

# ANGELS OF LEGEND

Sometimes, I feel that I will
never become a great saint,
what with all these people around
with their
thoughts and needs
and complaints and minds.

Then, I remember that
saints lived on Earth,
not that tropical island
the mind calls heaven,

And that these people
are the angels of legend
sent here
to keep me
awake.

# MAID FOR THIS

The cleaning is exhausting.
I agree.

The hatred, violence, apathy,
corruption…

They just
keep piling up.

Every morning,
billions of thought generators
come online,
the most complex processors
in the known universe,

Powerful enough to decipher
the inner workings of stars

But are instead used to
spew boiling, hot garbage all over
this world.

It's enough to make the
heartiest lover
anemic.

Those who see only darkness
cannot see the sun.
Those who ignore darkness
are blinded by false light.

Don't wait for someone else.
Remember, when facing such filth,
that you,
you
are the
maid for this.

Disinfecting creation
from illusion,

Holding awareness
in your palm like
a broom.

# THE HEART REPLIES

The ego says, "Go ahead,
write something clever."

The heart just laughs.

"What's so funny?" asks the
ego. To which the heart replies,

"You think your finite wit will
capture the attention of the world,
but

"Attention lies in the heart

"And you don't speak the language."

# MOST WILLING
# ACCOMPLICE

Look the entire history of human
stress in the eye
and you'll find the words

*I want.*

Now, if want is not the mastermind

It is definitely
the most willing
accomplice.

# CHOICE AS A WAVE

It is important to remember
in this life

That we have about as much choice
as a wave.

With all our growth,
our stretching,
and striving,

Everything we have done—
our kindness, our sins,
our compassion, our selfishness—

Could never ever separate us
from the ocean.

# A NEW REALITY

Sometimes, when fear arises
we rush to get away from him,
to avoid him,
to sedate him.

Instead, lovers,
we must sit with him,
surrender to him,
feel where he has entered
the body,

Honor him,
bless him,
merge with him,
and watch him dissipate.

Then, and only then, can we correctly
use the information
he has left us
to birth a new reality.

I know, I know,
these words are not proper
poetry.

But the prescribed action
plan
most certainly
is.

# YOUR BLESSED
# GAZE

Don't jump for stars.
They are a long distance
away
by design.

And if you spend the time,
the effort,
to reach them,

Build the vehicle.
Jump through
the celestial hoops

And actually get near one.

You may find
that their nature
is to burn.

They consume all smaller
bodies in their
wake with an
unparalleled ferocity.

Their warmth
is a by-product
of their appetite
for consumption.

This, dear one,
is why they shine.

Instead of stretching
across the great expanse,

Reach inside
of yourself,
and you will find

The sacred flame
that illumines
the entire universe.

And the stars,
at the slightest hint of
your blessed gaze,

Will bow to you
in worship.

# CAST THEM OFF

Dear one, there is no crevice,
no corner,
no peninsula,
no island

Where you can hide your greatness from yourself.

The mind will send storm clouds
to blind you from your excellence.

But do not fret.
These are temporary.

Sometimes, we get accustomed to our rain boots and umbrellas.

But we can cast them off

And let our inner radiance
shine through.

You have so much to offer.
Give yourself the freedom to make mistakes.

And through your progress, you will find
that within your heart
lies the most elusive perfection,

And a sense of trust,
peace, and excitement will permeate
every task.

# AMATEUR NIGHT

We all bought tickets
from a scalper
to see the
mind
live on stage.

The price for admission?
Our
attention.

And we each
paid in full.

We take temporary delight
watching the understudy
belt out a few notes

When all the while
the One
we are dying to meet
is backstage.

# DO NOT FOLLOW THEM

For some, life is a
white picket fence,
defined more
by what it keeps out
than what it contains.

Do not follow them.

The heart will say,
"Something's not right
here.

"That picket is meant for piercing.
Look at its shape!"

For some,
uniformity
is enticing,

as if Mother Earth
wanted only one type of child.

Do not follow them.

They are caught
between life
and the idea of life.

The lovers will say,
"Something's not right here.
Something is missing."

Absence fills a space
faster than abundance,
and it paints the walls
with want.

For some, life ends
just beyond the boundary
of sameness.

Do not follow them.

From a distance,
you'll see prison bars
where they see only
safety.

Pretty masks often
conceal painful realities

So good people
can't tell the difference
between freedom and fear,
exclusivity and exclusion.

Some ways of living
are threatened
by love.

Do not follow them.

# THERE IS NO DEMOCRACY HERE

The pupil is the gatekeeper.
Its sole function
is to determine how much
light gets in.

Clearly, the guards have a thing for you.

Oh, what the sight of a
beautiful woman does to a man!
Behold this slave to longing.

One should be careful.
Desire moves
in such a way
as to inspire corruption.

The votes
to love you forever
or leave this place
have been tallied.

Landslides
often signal an
emerging dictatorship.

There is no democracy here.

I am hopeless.
Like a tree who needs the ground
but wants the air,
I will reach for you until
they cut me down.

I need to be close to you,
closer than the light
that is inside your cells.

Have I created this life, or has it been given to me?
Have we created love, or are we sharing it?

What madman issued the order
to paint the air with your essence?

Where can I go that you are not with me?

What am I other than the pulse of love that beats between us?

Nothing matters except your lips.
When they open, all logic and distraction die.

Have pity on this hopeless soul.
No choice now but to close my eyes,
and disappear.

When there is no distinguishing
between you and me,
all that's left
is love.

# LISTEN

All day, people mill
about, asking the wrong
questions.

They ask, "What would you do
if the vault door swung open
and all your obstacles dissolved in
the wind?"

The sage prefers to ask,
"If the Beloved blew out the
majestic sky candle
and erased the moon,

"If this were the last
breath to enter the
lungs of eternity,

"What would you,
how would you,
who would you
be?"

For that's who you are
before you ever were.

And the ear in your heart,
which still hears
the falcon sing,
is begging you to
listen.

# LADY BIRD

There is a fire in
my lungs when the
lady bird breathes.

Ecstasy is the
forgotten language of
being.

Cells quiver
from head to toe.
There is only opening.
There is the endless sense of more.

There is a fire is my
lungs that cannot be doused,
flames that have burned for all
eternity

When the lady bird
breathes her precious song.
OHM.

# ONCE YOU STOP PLAYING

Mind says,
"Peace is a goal.
And like all goals,
it requires hard work,
a heavy lift,
to make it manifest,
to make it real."

Heart says,
"Peace is a game
of hide-and-seek.
Once you stop playing,
your opponent will sit down
beside you and ask,
'Well, friend, what should we do now?'"

Once you give up the chase,
the unobtainable
will reveal itself
as your faithful playmate,
your constant companion,

who has been patiently waiting
for you to pause
just long enough
to take notice.

# THE RECORD

For the record,
Each and
every time
someone uses
an eraser,

A million angels burst
into fits
of laughter,

Musing at how mortals
could possibly believe
that any precious
moment of learning

Could ever be
considered unworthy
of a page in the
book of love.

# BEFORE THEIR
# LIGHTS GO OUT

All the way here you came
to their doorstep,
braving the self-inflicted traffic
jamming your life with duty.

Their fragrance,
grace,
descended on your ignorance.

Again and again,
you returned,

Forgetting the tears,
the turmoil,
caused by their fire.

They are scattered,
these great ones,

Littered all over the sky
with a great expanse of living
nothingness between them,

Light years apart from
one another.

But if you ever
sat at the feet of true suns
when their bodies burned
with life,

You'd be wise not to stray
too far.

Organize your entire orbit
around them while
you can.

Let their holy flame
devour you
and turn you into
Him

Before their lights go out.

# FORTY-SECOND WEEK

I will not stray
tonight.

Food and drink
have lost their
magic.

The furnace in my belly
scorched my heart
and mercilessly engulfed
my mind

All because the Beloved stopped by
with blouse undone,
raised an eyebrow like the crescent
moon,

And blew me a kiss.

Now I lie on the floor,
screaming courageously

Like a pregnant woman in her
forty-second week

Who will not rest
until she holds
proof
of
God.

# THE GIFT OF PARENTING

The gift of parenting is the effortless way
in which our children force us
to face our inner tyrant

Who would have,
who could have,
otherwise remained
hidden.

# E JOY OF
# RRENDER

eaf's greatest joy
when it blazes bright green and independent.

ts greatest joy is when it surrenders fully to the great invisible
from which it came,

n it becomes so full that it changes color and is barely recog-
le to its kin.

finally, in love,

# WHAT THE BOY
# SEES

Do you see what the boy
sees?

Building mansions for the rich
while living in poverty.

Do you see what the boy
sees?

Men who
lay claim to heaven
while trading their wings
in an unholy exchange.

Do you see what the boy
sees?

The powerful make friends
with the powerful;
the poor make love to pain.

Do you feel what the boy
feels?

Beyond desire, want, or
delusions of purpose,

The absolute necessity
of the
kingdom of love,

As vital as air,
as essential as water.

Comfort
so foreign to his mind-scape,

Unrest in every temple
save the one
in his heart.

If you see what the boy sees,
you just may become
the one

Whom your soul
has been waiting for

To ring the alarm
and wake us from
the dream
of the world.

Open
your
eyes.

# ALL THE MEDALS

You think one bird flies
higher than another?
Have you not seen the
shape of the world?

What is height to an infinite sky
but mortal vanity?

We compete with each
other and
end up at
the exact same distance
from the sun.

We are made of earth
yet scared of sharing
when our bones
belong to the ground.

Why race?
History shows
the maggots
hold all the medals.

Just one more
undeniably
glorious reason
to love.

# CHAMPION LOVER

When you meet difficulty,
merge with it.
When the ego goes,
so goes the difficulty.

What is love?
The whip that breaks pride.

Its precise handling
births dissolution.

When the ego dissolves,
the whip is but a breeze
for the lilies of the field.

When the ego is present,
catastrophic wounds.


Today, a mouse dreamed of
being a world-class sprinter,
so the Beloved sent
its forefathers a cat.

Reason is the ego's last
hiding place.

Come out, come out,
wherever you are.


The champion lover
merges
with the whip,

Surrenders it all

For one chance to
kiss the
skilled hands
that hold it.

# POWER OF LOVE

Contraction is the result
of the power of love.

Whether it's the womb,
a star,
old age,
an orgasm,

Nothing expands forever.

Eventually,
the distance between
you and love
becomes unbearable.

So, we close
the book on illusion
and collapse
back into the
self.

We collapse
back into God.

# LOVE LIKE THIS

She continues,
so amazing is She.
Independent of any imaginable form,
She is the mother of imagination.

Like a centipede,
who was once a man
so in love with Her
that he vowed to kiss the
ground of being
one hundred times with each step.

Only the brave
love like this.

Many say they stand
for love.

Only a few
are truly willing
to fall.

# KINDRED SPIRIT
# WOLF

Reader, beware.

The wolf
has pierced my pen.

Not the wolf of rage,
the wolf of spirit.

My pack,
the planets,

On the hunt for
eternity.

In the summer,
I shed,
leaving traces
of love.

I am winter.

I serenade the moon.
She understands cold,
distance, and longing.

That which animates her
burns miles away.

That which animates her
illuminates us all.

Don't track me
unless you can
match my hunger.

Don't track me
unless you
crave the infinite.

One glance, and
my words will
tear the flesh
off forgetfulness.

Ignorance has no
place to hide.

You'll find no
safety around me,
save the parts
of you
that are kin.

# WHEN THE DAY COMES

Even the sun rotates.

Nothing in the universe
remains still.

Let me restate this
for lovers.

Nothing that hears
the one verse can
possibly remain
still.

Even dark matter moves
with each note.

I share this so that when
the day comes,

When your soul
is aged
to perfection,

When you start twirling
incessantly,

You won't think yourself mad.

Instead, you will trust
that your inner ear
is finely tuned
for elegance.

# THE TRUE SYMPHONY

To read Tagore,
to read Rabia,
is like listening to Mozart.

To live Rumi,
to live Hafiz,
is to become Beethoven's piano.

To be pounded on mercilessly
by God,

Belting incomprehensible notes
until one is emptied of all stubbornness
and the true symphony is born.

The wise listen,
the supreme become.

# LIFE AFTER LIFE

I don't know why I love you.
Anything I can point to,
any physical aspect or mental concept of you,
is impermanent.

Nothing I can think of will remain tomorrow.
I cannot even prove in any tangible way
that the love I profess is real,
because I am the experiencer.

I cannot hold it in my hand or measure it.
It cannot be seen or touched.

I love you because your existence has reminded me—has revealed—
this once-hidden, unexplainable, living, breathing mystery of love
within me.

In fact, the words *I* and *you*
don't make sense around the word *love*.
Love is too big to be bordered by persona.
Truth cannot be contained by illusion.
That is why I love you,
because for some unknown reason,

boundless love arose within my chest the moment I saw you.
And I have been slowly awakening to this reality
with each passing day.

One should be eternally grateful to any person
who willingly or unknowingly gives such a gift.
I love you because
love slowly erases *you* and *I* until only itself remains.
And yet somehow, therein lies the mystery.
It somehow lets us live to experience it.
We are completely gone,
annihilated, no more,
and yet very much alive.

Life after life.
I want to experience this
with you.

# UNIQUELY YOU

If you've ever held a baby,
then you know we come into this
world
with something,

Something uniquely us,

Something beyond wiring
that registers joy at the smell
of mother's milk,

Something akin to brilliance brewing
before the first word,

Some hidden strength that propels
growth.

Value yourself,
because there is something precious
within you that is untainted by
experience and unconcerned with
time,

Something uniquely you
that's
too large ever to be categorized
and
far too gorgeous
to be named.

# HEARING THEM SPEAK

Certainty
is the father of debate.

Possibility
is the mother of conversation.

These two children
are never in the same class.

One
is always closing the door;

The other,
opening.

Friends,
why argue over the
form longing
takes?

This will only make the
flowers wilt,
when there is enough sunshine
for the entire garden.

When one's mind
is open to possibility,

Hearing them speak
is like watching
an angel
paint the sunrise
with a song.

# PSA

The following is a
public service announcement.

Doctors, you are
hereby ordered to
administer mandatory
eye exams
for all those
who trade love
for religion.

Revoke their licenses.
Confiscate their car keys.
You'd be doing them a favor.

Ban them from your boardrooms,
court houses, and all decision-making
posts,

Or else you may find them
on a warm night
at a bar with the enemy,
contract in hand,

Happily
pawning off all
our country's
water and air
for one shiny bar of gold.

# RAMBLINGS

Sometimes, it's an image.
Sometimes, it's a word.

I grow weary of long days when I have lost sight of you.

I measure every interaction
by counting the number of veils
hanging between me and ecstasy.

Idiotic questions
fueled by fear
arise.

Will the sun cast us off into space?

The nonsense ramblings of a blind man!

The sun's embrace has held us this long.

Beware that kind of love.

No. She will not let us go.

When her passion rises, she will devour us, making us one with her.

True love's form has no function but annihilation.

When the heat rises,
it will bring this whole thing to a close.
It will bring each and every
one of us
home.

# SUNLIGHT FOR SAINTS

Take a bath in Whitman.
Brush your teeth with Dogen.

Walk to work with Al-Hallaj
and labor with Jesus.

Eat lunch with Meister Eckhart
and Eckhart Tolle.

Spend the afternoon
within the lungs of existence,
chasing the breath of Mary and Khadijah.

Dine with Baldwin.
Have dessert with Giovanni.

Take an evening stroll with Thurman
and let Angelou tuck you in.

That which makes the stars burn
goes unscathed by fire.

Remember,
all sunlight is for saints,
and moonbeams are for birthing.

Fill your nightgown with love.

We were sent here to hear the sound of Ram when he first caught
the scent of Sita.

Let peace rock your infancy to sleep and yearning awaken your
true form
once and
for
all.

# WE SPOKE OF YOU

Light was my dinner guest for the evening.
I do hate to dine alone.

I thought of making small talk,
perhaps about the weather.

But how does one complain about a child to the mother?

So, instead, we spoke of you.
And Light said the strangest thing.
"When you speak of her, I see my mother in your eyes.

"When you speak this way, I wish to curl up in Love's arms, nurse
from her bosom, and be cradled
to sleep once again
like she did when I was young,

"Before I got too big,
before Mom told
the universe to
breathe."

# SOUL'S BELLY

A funnel filled with honey
drips one drop at a time
deep into my soul's belly
each time I look at you.

My mouth opens,
not believing
that such beauty could
stand alone.

Your hips
make a mockery of abstinence.

You are the reason that eyes are never born far away
from mouths and hands.

And like a great, hungry bear, I stand
awake for the first time in months,
gazing at you in complete amazement,

Thinking,
"How can I keep you alive forever
and still devour you?"

For nothing so gorgeous can possibly remain separate
without meeting the fire of my hunger,

Without merging with me
forever
in
love.

# MY SHATTERED LIFE

Help!
Thief!

I was robbed yesterday
in broad daylight.

Anger—
Anger stole my integrity.

While the sun was high,
darkness crept in.

My words were stolen;
my tongue, extorted.

The evidence:
my shattered life.

Like empty drawers hurled
recklessly on the floor,
mocking me.

Priceless and irreplaceable.

"Call the police," you say.
But why?

Punishment is the least
effective change agent.

It only drives anger
deeper into hiding.

No, the police can't help.
I need a true authority.

Forgiveness—
Forgiveness is the only
detective that can catch
anger.

Be forewarned.
This arrangement
is not for the weak.

When forgiveness and anger meet,
it's like pouring alcohol
on an open wound.

Fire, baby!

It burns,
but it heals.

Now, friends,
if, like me,
this has happened to you

And you feel that this
is unfair,

That you don't deserve
such a burning

Because you are the victim, not the criminal, after all,

This is OK.
It simply means
that you are not ready.

But when you are,
since you are my friend
and I know forgiveness,
I will give you her number.

I will even hold your hand
and wipe your tears
while the Beloved grabs ahold
of your tender, open wound
and pours.

# TRIUMPH

Beloved, You should do this,
not me.
You should say this,
not me.

One look at their anguish,
and I will cease.

I will melt like
ice in the sun.

I will spread like
pollen in the midday wind.

Such courage is reserved
for braver souls than me.

A painting of the sunset
is not the sunset.

In the same way, words
cannot capture death.

But how, Beloved?
How is Your sunset built?
If it is true that there is no light out there,
no color independent of our eyes
and brains,

If it be true that
nothing exists the way we perceive it
without our perception tools,

Then we are somehow connected,
creative forces in this field of You.

Let us now cocreate here.

From our anguish,
from our grief,
from each dropping tear
on Your fertile palm,

Let us raise an army of lovers
on this earth
fueled by the remembrance
of our beloved friend.

She mothered all she knew,
so let each heart see her sons
as their own.

Let each heart see her husband
as their own.

Let each heart see her friends
as their own.

Let the alchemy of rebirth confirm
our majestic origin.

Beloved,
we did not create eternal
love.

Yet through Your generosity,
it is our greatest triumph,
our victory horn.

Let it sound a warning
to the farthest star.

Our great friend
has come home.

# THE HARDEST WORK

Dear one,
you look tired this morning,
as if you walked across
the universe,
squeezed candle wax out of
your own veins,
and lit the sun,

As if you just
untied the rope
tethered from your waist
to Earth
so that you alone could drag
it around the heavens.

But
you
didn't.

All you've done
is open your eyes.

So, rejoice.
The hardest work
has already
been done
for
you.

And there is not a
drop of debt to repay.

# COLOR GAMES

Split one light
into different boxes.

This one's for you.
This is for me.

Chop it further with the
sword of preference.

Blue for thou.
Red for thee.

Tell stories of their
unique greatness,

Songs of glory
and revelry.

Through much pride,
separation solidified

Them from us,
he from we.

Conflict seems
the way of things.

No peace found in
diversity.

And we still play
these color games.

Pain shines through
our history.

But the light was
never
truly split.

It just slowed down
so we could see

The complete spectrum,
its majestic range,

The beauty within
its unity.

# PATIENTLY

My father didn't know
his father.
They never met.

Instead, my father met
his soul,
and his soul taught
him how to love.

And he waited his whole
life
patiently
to share that lesson with me.

Sometimes, it happens that way.
The Beloved turns emptiness
into a sun,

And that sun waits
patiently
for the right world

To share its light.

# A PEASANT COLLECTION

The disciple said,
"Enough poetry, master.
Give it to me straight.
What does the future hold?"

The master replied,

"The wine is in the being;
doing alone holds no juice.

"Being while doing
is the walk of the
free.

"It is the path of the
saints,

"The heart of the yogi.

"For the doers,
the future is
a cluttered box
filled with
endless distraction;

"A gathering of ideas
and accomplishments,
regrets, and fears;

"A peasant collection
that breeds exhaustion
and robs one of true wealth.

"But for the wise beings,
the future is
a contract with the infinite
carved out of the here and now
and sealed with gratitude.
It is a blueprint of possibility,
an endless string of cocreation
that is possible only when one lives
with the constant awareness and
experience of this
eternal moment.

"It is like the breath
whose every move
is blessed
by its
intention
to love.

"So, young one,
what does the future hold?

"Everything
that you hold
most dear
right
now."

# WORST BARGAIN

We are wired for joy,
but we settle for pleasure.

This

Is the
worst
bargain.


Poor choices
stretch out
like roots
underneath the ground
of our lives,

Growing bad-habit
trees

That sprout up
everywhere,

Choking the sky

And blocking our
view of the
sun.

You must
negotiate harder!

Meditate.
Pray.
Be still

Until the
salesman
tells you
the whole truth
about the lemon
he calls a car,

Until the
sales rep
sees that you
cannot be swayed,
enticed, or convinced
that true happiness
lies in the driver's seat
of the next shiny thing.

Then, the most
miraculous thing will
happen.

He will take
off his blazer,
resign his post,

And finally come
to work for
you

And direct
all his talents
toward finding
that
which you truly
seek,

Toward discovering
who
and what
you really are.

# LOVE'S BIDDING

The rules are simple.
Every single woman
is someone's
daughter.
Every single man
is someone's
son.

When they meet trouble,
feel their parents' pain,
the sadness,
the despair,
the raw terror.

Don't flee from this.
Embrace it.
Meditate on it.
Let it surround you
until there is but
a pit of agony
where your stomach
once was;
until you lose sight
of the four directions;

Until your life
is so consumed
by prayers
for their safe return,
for compassion,
for light,
and for warmth
that you forget
they are not your kin.


Then, while the
bloodlines are blurred,
get
up
off your comfortable cushions,
your boardroom chairs,
your seats of separation

and go out into the world
and do love's bidding.

# THE HUNT

Be a good bloodhound,

Nose to the ground,
hot on the trail
left behind by love.

Leave one nostril fixed
on the scent of bliss,
the other
on the fragrance of forgetfulness.
This will aid in discernment

And keep you sober enough
to sniff out the joy in
everyone,

Even if they can
no longer smell
it within themselves.

# ENDURANCE

The only difference
between you
and a perfect one:

Endurance.

You have both
taken an oath.

You have both
failed to keep it
one hundred times a day,

Only to take it again.

You both know that at
the heart of
this oath
lies a prayer:

"Help me be more loving."

Look in the eyes of a
perfect one.

You'll see a life
courageous enough
to have suffered its
own failure
over and over
again

While kneeling
naked and exposed
in the boiling
light of day.

Never
give
up.

# A LITTLE ROOM

Your belly is already full.
There is no benefit
to piling on.

Satiation
is the casket nail;

Addiction, the hammer.

Numbness masquerades
as satisfaction
for a spell.

But when he disrobes,
Lovers lie disappointed.

Alchemy requires breathing
room.

Space
fuels the fire

So the unifier can
do its work

Churning food into
the body.

Hunger
fans the flame

So the hidden one
can
be felt

Carving food out
of earth,

Crafting you out
of food.

So, leave a little room,
dear ones.

Just a little room
in life

For this
sacred
magic.

# SEE LOVE

It's quite simple, really.

We bought tickets to
see love.
Justice is merely the opening act.

They're playing for one lifetime only,
so tonight's the night.

We've waited
far too long.
The show has started.

Now,
let
us
in.

# THE GREATEST TRICK

There was a magician,
a great alchemist
known throughout the land.

His powers were formidable.

One day, the king
sent for him.

When he arrived at the gate of
the castle,
he was rushed to the king's quarters.

The king said,
"Thank you for coming.

"My son is beyond reproach.
He was captured by my enemy,
and for a time he was tortured
in the most unspeakable ways.

"Now he spends his
time alone. When approached,
he becomes violent and murderous.
He speaks only foul, cursed words.
And he has the look of the devil in his eyes.

"Can you use your powers to help him?"

The magician said, "I am not a doctor, sire."
To which the king replied,
"Doctors are no use. They won't go near him for fear of death."

The magician thought for a moment.
He could tell that the king truly loved his son.

"Bring the prince to me," said the magician.
"And bring a bowl of acid."

Within moments,
armed guards returned
with the prince.
He was truly a wretched sight.

The magician said,
"Do you know me?"

The prince said, "Yes.
And my father is a fool if he thinks a showman can help me. If these
guards release me, I will cut the life from you for wasting my time."

"That's a pity," said the magician.
"Then you would miss my final act,
the greatest trick ever witnessed.

"For I
will turn acid into honey.
And you will assist me."

The prince was mildly curious.
"Carry on, then."

So, the magician held the bowl out toward the prince and said,

"I want you to take this bowl of acid
and throw it in my face."

The prince said, "Father, I thought he was a magician, not a jester.
Don't be a fool.
I will do it."

The king looked deeply concerned.

The magician looked still and committed.

The guards released the prince, who tested the acid with his finger-
tip and winced in pain.

"It is real, sire," said the magician. "Now, grab ahold of it and throw
it in my face."

The prince hesitated.

The magician chanted, "Compassion is for the weak." It was the war cry of the enemy kingdom. This enraged the prince, and he took the bait.

"Do it. Do it now," said the magician.

The prince threw the bowl of acid in his face. The magician's screams of pain filled the kingdom. His face was bloody, and he could barely breathe.

The prince was mortified. He cried out. "What is the purpose of this madness?"

The magician, with barely the strength to breathe, uttered,

"I must now say the magic words."

"What magic words?" asked the prince, who held him in his arms.

The magician looked straight into his eyes and said,

"I forgive you."

# CARRY
# SOMETHING

The curse of guilt
is that you will
carry something
every day
of your life.

The gift is that
you can choose whether
to carry the shame
or the blessing.

# THIS, TOO

You exist in every story.

Look deeply
and find
yourself there.

There is no plotline
in existence
that hasn't already
played out
in your cells.

When you look
in the mirror,
do you see the
Beloved's clothing
staring back?

The world is Her closet.
Each encounter,
each character,
is but a wardrobe change.

Freedom lives
everywhere,

Connects everything,
and has
no known
address.

Your enemies
do a
noble work.

They are written in
to find an
unprotected
thread
and
tug.

They do it for you
when it is far
too difficult
to unravel
yourself,

Too challenging
to live in
everyone
as everyone.

They teach essence.

This, too,
is
love.

# COURTROOM OF
# THE REAL

Does it bother you?

What?

That you'll never know
what the earth looks like
when you are not looking
at it.

You'll never know
what she sounds like
when you are not the
one hearing her song.

In the courtroom of
the real,

Memory is insufficient
evidence.

It's great
for finding everything
except the truth.

How can you be certain
about the fossil
you held yesterday
when today your hand is different?

Angels often
masquerade as sunbeams.

But when these thoughts arise,

They come out of hiding
and whisper,
"You didn't create the world.

You're creating it."

And the joy in my heart
grows so heavy
that I fall to my knees
and weep.

# INANE BABBLE

When
you follow direction,

Follow as if
it comes from above.

When
you give direction,

Speak like you
would to love's
neighbor

Who would
gladly cross
the fence

To vent about
the unkind and
the impostors
over tea
and homemade pie.

When given direction,
remember,
the word *when*
implies choice.

If someone barked
orders in their sleep,

Would you follow their
inane babble?

Most leadership should
be regarded this way.

Similarly,
when soldiers
seek pardon for
"just doing their job,"

A thorough jury will ponder,

"Could they not see that their
general was asleep?"

If you long for the
ocean,

Keep the company of
fish,

For whom
separation is death.

They know the difference
between living

And simply gasping
for air.

Fish die
in and out of
water.

Which do you think
they prefer?

Follow those
who have chosen
to live in
the natural state
of love.

They were handcrafted
to lead you home.

# HOW LONG MUST WE WAIT?

How long must we wait?
How long will you hide your secret identity from the world?

The love in you
is the root cause
of everything.

You've done the training.
Now, join the front.

Forget perfection.

The world
doesn't need another
great savior.

No,
what the world
needs is the
transformative power
of
great love.

# SOME INMATES

Love is held prisoner
by your
self-loathing.

What a waste of thoughts!

It's your addiction to stress
that causes stress.
Nothing else.

Only disease does this,
makes people complain
about every gift
they've been given,
turns everything
once desired
into pain.

Some inmates, when
given a hammer,
will erect more bars
when there's a wall
to smash behind them,

when there's a new day
just waiting for them
if they would simply turn around.

It's good to get
straight talk from
a page.

That way, there is
no one
to be cross with.

So, energy
can be conserved
for planting
words that take root.

And should
they sprout inside you
as if they were your own,
then trust
that they are growing
in the direction of truth.

# I'VE BEEN THERE

If my eyes have changed,
it's because
I've been there

In a room
surrounded by souls
present to great love.

Not mere observers
but impassioned participants.

Where the carpet,
the walls, the air,
the elements
pulsate
to serve the beating heart.

If my eyes have changed,
it's because
I've been there

Where, try as they might,
all anyone can think of
is how much they love you.

Where words are spoken
not to convey meaning
but to pollinate the air
with joy.

Where the line
between friend and family
is obliterated.

If my eyes have changed,
it's because the journey
between my head and my heart
has finally ended

And words no longer suffice
to explain
the tenderness
found

Alive
and waiting.

If my eyes have changed,
then grab this old man's
hand

And I'll tell you a tale.
Not of what could be

But of what already

Always

Is.

# UNBLEMISHED IDEAL

If you're searching for perfection,
you'd best find a way to look into my heart.

You won't find it in my history,
my thoughts,
my words,
or my actions,

for these are but hollow echoes
of the unblemished ideal,
singing within the soul of me.

# SUFFERING

Only
the
selfish

Can be
bored
in a
world

With
so
much
suffering.

# SPEAK TRUE

You stand alone,
naked,
starved with thirst.

Your bare feet are charred.
The terrain
rough,
dry, and unforgiving.

Through many rising suns,
you have walked.

Suddenly, a wolf materializes.
Long has been its approach.

"How is it that you've come?"
you ask the mighty wolf.
"Of you, I have seen no equal,
and certainly not in a desert
like this.

"How is it that you appear so
strong and well fed?

"How long have you followed?"

The wolf says, "I have followed since
your mother and father
lost themselves in sense pleasure,

"Since the great you collapsed into form."

You ask, "By what means have you followed?
What sense have you used to track me?"

"The sense of smell."

"Do you smell the body?"

"I smell the soul."

"Lies!
Wolf, you lie!

"No earthly nose
can detect
the eternal fragrance.

"What is it you smell?

"Speak true or perish."
You pick up a stick and a rock.

The wolf grows larger.

You drop the rock.
The wolf shrinks.

You drop the stick.
The wolf shrinks further still.

This is the moment of wisdom.

"Wolf," you say.
"Speak true."

"It is fear you smell.
It is the fear of death that enlivens
your nostrils."

"True," the wolf says,
bowing his head.

"Then I shall fear no more," you say.
"I shall be done with fear forever.

"Be gone now, great wolf.
Travel onward and
do for others
what you have done for me."

# CUTEST LITTLE SIGN

My daughter is going
through changes.

Rebellion
is
high.

How do I raise her?

I was raised
by my parents
who were raised by
my grandparents
who were raised by
my ancestors
who were raised by
slavery.

My mind,
the whip.
This life,
my back.

Discipline is a
mask
that fits
so comfortably
over the face
of bondage

When right before me
points
the cutest
little sign

Reading,
"This way.
This way
to freedom."

# BACK AT ME

Every morning,
I sit
just to get a glimpse
of you,

Hoping that,
in the darkness,
I might see your eyes

Staring from inside me

So that as the day
begins,
I might recognize
your face
staring back at me
from everywhere at once.

# THINK OF THAT

Even the sun,
as important as it is,
returns home
when the time comes.

Think of that.
Giving your all
to the lives
of others

And then,
when called,
letting it all go
in a
flash.

That, dear ones,
is the stuff
we are made of.

# COSMIC JOY
# GENERATOR

Is it possible
that the reason for all
this—
this life—

Is the joy of revelation?

Is it possible
that the only joy
Shiva couldn't experience
was remembering himself
due to his own
omniscience,

So, She cooked up a way
to forget
simply for the joy
of remembering
And is living that joy
through us?
If so,

our enlightenment is
a kind of
cosmic joy generator.

Or

Is it that his primary joy
is creating more of himself
out of sheer will

And that the dance of concealment and revealment is somehow a
crucial ingredient in the recipe for creating God? Without this,
would something be missing?
Perhaps more salt or butter?

I have no idea.
But I wonder…

# GUIDANCE AND FUEL

Don't misunderstand anger.
It arises whenever
there is a perceived
lack of love
in the world.

It is energized information.
It is guidance and fuel
intelligently designed
to help you get up
and find
love.

# INTERIOR DESIGN

It would appear
that the Beloved's
favorite
paint color is
family,

For She has applied
generous coats of it
on the walls of
every room in Her
home.

This bears repeating.

She has applied
generous coats of it
on the skin
of every person
in this world.

Few people
cultivate an
eye for such things.

So few
appreciate
the flow
of Her
interior design.

# TO YOUNG MEN

You were born
of a woman

To embody her essence.

Your frame is muscular
to bear the weight
of her compassion.
The longer you carry it,
the stronger
you grow.

You'll live in
this world
that values
what you know.

You'll leave this life
valuing what you feel.

Live
like you've already left.

That
which you emanate from
is in the room with you.
Therein lies the magic.

To ambition,
these words
are a waste.

But
they redirect light
from the stage
to the
self.

They shift attention
from the character
to the script.

In the hidden
economy,
what you produce
is worth
less
than
how you love.

What else is there
to say
to young men?

# ENDS WELL

Life is a love story
that, for the ego,

Never ends well.

# THE SLEEP OF
# OTHER

When will we wake up from
the sleep of other?

When will we expand our sphere of compassion to include every-
one or, better yet, dissolve its circumference altogether to exclude
no one?

Our sword of discrimination was not meant to be turned on one
another.
It was meant to be used on ourselves
to slice a line between our highest selves and the thoughts/actions
that blind us to the illusion of separation.

Many of us were raised in the darkness of segregation because our
parents were still living by lessons that should have died with their
teachers.

A seed loves only the dark-brown soil. It feels safe and believes it
knows all it needs to know. Tell the seed that a few feet away there
is blazing sunlight and plants to love that grow above the earth in
every color imaginable. Tell it that there are flying creatures to love
that live to visit them and spread their essence all over the globe.
Tell it that by expanding its love, it will grow into something of

unfathomable beauty. Further, tell it that its growth in love not only will serve the entire planet but also is a necessary ingredient for life itself. And it will think that you are mad. It is safe and small. And what you propose sounds dangerous and crazy. It likes its neighborhood. It doesn't want intruders. It doesn't want to leave, and it doesn't care to think about the outside world.

This is what darkness does. It lulls us to sleep, limits our perception, and makes us susceptible to erroneous beliefs about the world at large and our role in it. Sure, it feels safe, but it is a casket unsuitable for the living.

One would hope that a former slave, if given the chance, would not enslave anyone else and that an actual living, breathing holocaust survivor wouldn't build a concentration camp with her own hands. Because they would see it for what it was. A human atrocity. An abomination.

But their grandkids might if they learn history the way we teach history. Sanitized.
Because instead of learning that greed, control, a lust for power, a lust for land, separation, race, racism, and the very notion of other are the enemy, they would learn that some really bad men lived a long time ago, and America with its flag and eagle got rid of them. Case closed. Chapter and verse. On to the next quiz. When all the while the real enemy is alive and laughing it up in the hearts and minds of every person on the planet. If we learned history within this context, we couldn't walk by ghettos or see people
being forcibly relocated or murdered by employees of the state without making connections to past pain.

So, we as a people are doomed to repeat the story. We just play different characters each time around.

We are asleep. We are watching a rerun, and we don't even know it because the set design has changed and the costumes are different. But the enemy, the notion of other, is still at large—a badass, murderous, gangsta Houdini, who has never been caught!

Some of us feel exempt. We are not involved. We didn't do it. And we are genuinely good to the people around us, the people we know.

But

Apathy is a serial killer.
Only compassion can detect where it will strike next.

It's a henchman, a shakedown artist hired by the notion of other, strolling around the neighborhood, knocking on shop doors. And our minds pay handsomely for protection from the crushing truth in our own hearts.

When will we wake up from the sleep of other?
When will we respect the order of things?
Humanity is our primary identity.
Ethnicity, nationality, religion, political parties, caste—these are secondary because humanity can live without them. The opposite does not hold true.

Our skin color was shaped through environmental forces. Yet this antiquated idea of race still shapes our world.

Religion was created for man, not man for religion.

When you see a person suffering, help.
If your secondary identities weaken your drive to assist, rest assured the sleep of other has you.

Babies born in the womb
don't turn around and sell the womb piece by piece
and then kill each other for the profits.
And yet this is how we treat the earth
that was given to us all for free.

If your secondary identity kills for land, and you sit on the silent sidelines,
your humanity numbed by the novocaine of "them and us,"
rest assured the sleep of other has you.

It's parricide, plain and simple.
Humanity is being killed by
the ideas it gave birth to
the planet, being killed
by humanity.

Yes, we were taught that our
differences mean something,

That our secondary identities
are real and worth killing for.

But our teachers were asleep,

Leaving us with the arduous task

Of waking up.

# TREASURE CHESTS

There are eight billion treasure chests on the planet.

Finding them is not the hard part;

It's getting them to open up to you.

Do your words
fortify the locks,
or are they keys?

# PORT BY PORT

I came here to learn how
to be more loving.

It's really the only reason to
go anywhere.

I came here to love those
who need to be loved.

And I will do this
port by port
until
there is no place left
to go.

# GET THE MATH RIGHT

Every view is diminished in your
absence.
Every meal is less flavorful,
like love unearths a passageway
to being
lost to the modern world.

Does your presence
add light?
Or does your absence
add darkness?
I can't get the math right.

# NEXT

It's true.
The most unlikely possibility
is true.

I heard it from the Great One Herself.
You can dissolve
all your transgressions,
all your crimes and injuries,

By dipping them in a bag of gratitude.

You can be absolved
of all your
criminal acts

By pouring the sum total
of your wisdom
and your love
into what you do
next.

43738971R00120